# COMPUTERS

**Troll Associates**

# COMPUTERS

by Francene Sabin

Illustrated by Joseph Veno

**Troll Associates**

Library of Congress Cataloging in Publication Data
Sabin, Francene.
   Computers.

   Summary: Traces the development of the electronic computer, which during a relatively short time has come to play a very important role in society.
   1. Computers—Juvenile literature. [1. Computers]
I. Veno, Joseph, ill. II. Title.
QA76.23.S23    1985        001.64         84-2708
ISBN 0-8167-0314-0 (lib. bdg.)
ISBN 0-8167-0315-9 (pbk.)


Copyright © 1985 by Troll Associates, Mahwah, New Jersey
All rights reserved. No part of this book may be used
or reproduced in any manner whatsoever without written
permission from the publisher.
Printed in the United States of America

10  9  8  7  6  5  4  3  2  1

Information about every baby born in North America and Western Europe is stored in a computer. Hospital records of illnesses, operations, and injuries are also computerized, or entered in computers. Census records counting a nation's population are computerized. So are income-tax returns, bank accounts, bills from stores and utility companies, driving, fishing, and hunting licenses, school records, and airline reservations.

The space shuttle and other complex machinery depend on computers in order to function properly. There are computers in schools, offices, factories, and private homes. There are even computers that play electronic games. Computers have become a highly important part of the modern world and are expected to become even more important in the future.

The electronic computer has been in existence only a short time. But the idea of a machine to simplify counting is very old. Perhaps the first calculating, or counting, device was the abacus.

The abacus was invented in Asia, about two thousand years ago. It has rows of beads that the user moves by hand to add, subtract, multiply, and divide numbers. Someone who is quite skilled with an abacus can do fast calculations. But it is a simple and relatively limited calculator.

The first step toward developing a real computer came in the seventeenth century, when a young Frenchman named Blaise Pascal invented a counting machine. Pascal's machine was run by gears. It could add and subtract and could carry numbers from one column to the next.

The next significant advance toward developing computers took place in the eighteenth century. It was an automatic textile loom invented by another Frenchman, Joseph Marie Jacquard. Though it wasn't a counting device, it made a great contribution to the field of computers. It used paper cards with information recorded on them by means of a system of holes. To some extent, punch cards can be traced to Jacquard's invention.

The nineteenth century brought more developments. Charles Babbage, an English mathematics professor, drew up plans for a digital computer. And Lady Augusta Lovelace, a talented amateur mathematician, devised a system of binary arithmetic, which is still used for computers.

Still later in the nineteenth century, an American, Dr. Herman Hollerith, devised an electrically driven computing machine. It was designed to tabulate the results of the United States census of 1890. Hollerith's machine used punch cards and a binary system of numbers. It did its job extremely well. Even though the U.S. population had grown since the 1880 census, it took only one third the time to calculate the 1890 census.

Computer technology continued to advance slowly. Then, in the 1940s, the first electronic computers were introduced. Leading the way was ENIAC, short for the Electronic Numerical Integrator and Computer. It was created by a group of engineers and mathematicians at the University of Pennsylvania. Since its invention, there have been huge advances in computer technology. Many of these were brought about by the demands of the space program. Others stemmed from the invention of miniaturized electronic components.

# Computer System
(Showing Input and Output units, as well as CPU Component units)

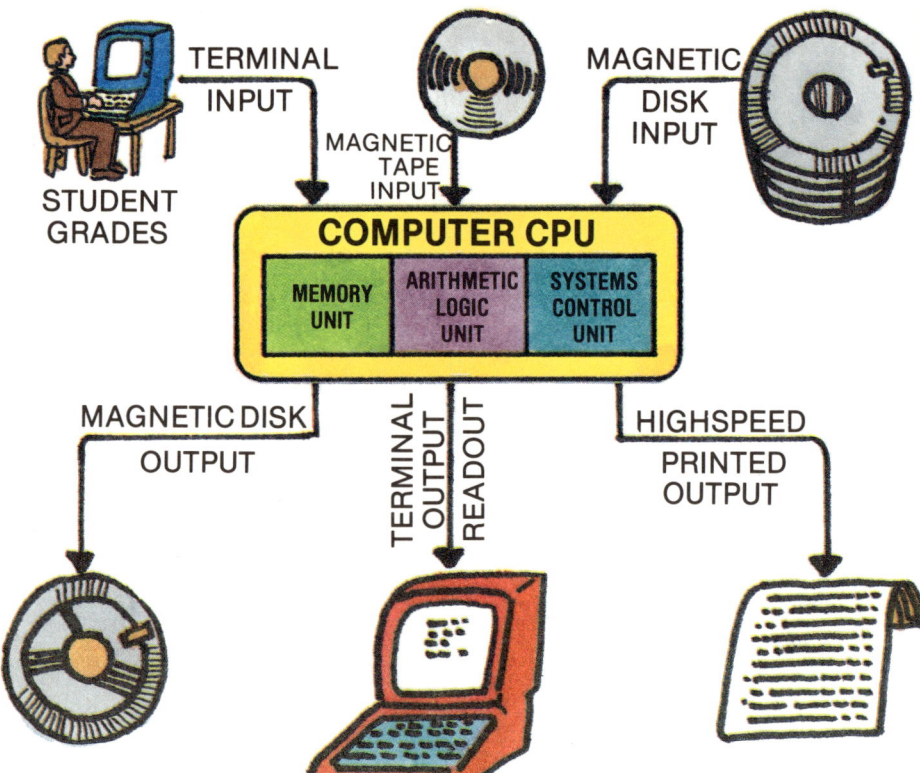

Modern electronic digital computers are made up of units. Each unit does a particular job. The input unit reads information, called data, that is fed into the computer. This data may be a list of names and addresses of people subscribing to a magazine. It may be mathematical calculations. It may be the scholastic records of everyone in your school. In fact, it may be about anything you can imagine.

The kind of data put into a computer depends on the needs of the user. For example, a department store feeds data about customer purchases and payments into its computer. Then decisions can be made about which merchandise to reorder and which customers owe money for something they have purchased.

The input unit of a computer also reads instructions. A set of computer instructions is called a program. A program tells a computer how to use the data that is being fed into it. A library program may tell a computer to find the names of all borrowers who have overdue books. The person who devises these instructions is called a programmer. The programmer writes the instructions in special computer language.

There are a number of computer languages. Some of these are called BASIC, FORTRAN, COBOL, and ALGOL. These names are a kind of abbreviation called an acronym. For example, COBOL is an acronym for COmmon Business Oriented Language, and FORTRAN is short for FORmula TRANslation. A computer then translates this language into machine language.

Machine language is a binary code, or two-digit code. It uses two different number symbols. These symbols are zero and one. How many zeroes and ones there are, and the order in which they are arranged, determine the letter or number they represent. For example, the symbols 1100 0001 mean the letter "A," the symbols 1100 0010 mean the letter "B," and so on. Each digit is called a bit. A modern, high-speed computer often holds many millions of bits.

The number code, or collection of bits, is recorded with electronic signals, which the computer counts. The part of the computer that does this counting is called the arithmetic/logic unit. The arithmetic/logic unit takes data from the storage unit, called the memory. Then, as it follows the program, it does the calculations it is instructed to do. When the calculations are completed, the answers are added to the computer's memory.

Those answers are now available for future use. The unit that delivers the answers is called the output. It produces information in a number of ways. One kind of output unit is like a high-speed printer. It produces information on paper called print-outs.

Many banks use computers to keep records of depositors' checking accounts. Statements of these accounts are sent to the depositors at regular intervals. The statements are often in the form of a computer print-out. The print-out shows the date and amount of every deposit made and every check written against the account. It also shows how much money is left in the account.

The output unit of a computer may also deliver its information in the form of magnetic tapes, disks, or as a display on a terminal or television screen, which is called a read-out. The output may also tell the answer out loud in electronic sounds that imitate the human voice.

# Computer Controller

He directs the data in
the CPU between the ALU, memory
and peripheral devices.

There are even some computers that produce spoken answers in a human voice. In order to do this, there first must be a collection of human voice recordings stored in the computer memory. The computer then selects the correct words from these recordings and plays them out loud.

All the parts of a computer depend on a key unit called the control. The control unit is like a teacher and a crossing guard combined. The control unit tells the computer which data to use and what to do with it. It also tells the computer how to deliver the answer. Furthermore, the control unit makes sure that operations are carried out smoothly, quickly, and in the right order.

Although a computer can perform very complicated operations, each step it takes is really very simple. It does not seem simple for two reasons. The first is that a computer works at a tremendous speed. The second reason is that it can handle more than one operation at a time.

Still, a computer is just a machine. It does only what it is programmed to do. Programmers or systems analysts use diagrams called flow charts to help them write programs that computers can follow. Each program is made up of a series of steps.

Each step depends on a yes or no answer to a simple question. If the answer is yes, the computer proceeds to the next step. If the answer is no, the computer must perform whatever operations are necessary to reach a yes answer. Only then can it go on to the next operation.

A computer performs its operations in a tiny fraction of a second. Furthermore, since it is a machine—without any feelings—it never gets bored. It will do the same operations over and over, millions of times if necessary, and never complain. Moreover, if it is functioning in good order, a computer will never make a mistake.

Sometimes a computer does turn out wrong answers. But they are seldom the fault of the machine. Most computer errors are really human errors. The program fed into the computer might be faulty, or the data fed into it might be faulty. Of course, there are occasional breakdowns in the computer itself, such as when a part wears out or breaks or when there is some disturbance with the machine's power source.

In a short time, electronic computers have revolutionized the way we gather information, store it, and use it. In the future, computers will have an even greater influence on our lives, on technology, indeed on virtually every phase of existence. Computers are unquestionably a major technological achievement of the twentieth century.